Meeting God At The Mall

Cycle C Sermons Based on Second Lessons for Advent, Christmas, and Epiphany

Mary Austin

CSS Publishing Company, Inc.
Lima, Ohio

MEETING GOD AT THE MALL
CYCLE C SERMONS BASED ON SECOND LESSONS FOR ADVENT,
CHRISTMAS, AND EPIPHANY

FIRST EDITION
Copyright © 2018
by CSS Publishing Co., Inc.

Library of Congress Cataloging-in-Publication Data
Names: Austin, Mary, 1954- author. Title: Meeting God at the mall : Cycle C sermons based on second lessons for Advent, Christmas, and Epiphany / Mary Austin. Description: First edition. I Lima, Ohio : CSS Publishing Company, Inc., [2018]
Identifiers: LCCN 2018031749 I ISBN 9780788029448 (paperback: alk. paper) I ISBN 0788029444 (paperback : alk. paper) I ISBN 9780788029455 (eBook) I ISBN 0788029452 (eBook)
Subjects: LCSH: Advent sermons. I Christmas sermons. I Epiphany--Sermons. I Sermons, American--21st century. I Church year sermons. I Common lectionary (1992). Year C. I LCGFT: Sermons.
Classification: LCC BV4254.3 .A97 2019 I DDC 252/.61--dc23
LC record available at https://lccn.loc.gov/2018031749

For more information about CSS Publishing Company resources, visit our website at www.csspub.com, email us at csr@csspub.com, or call (800) 241-4056.

e-book:
ISBN-13: 978-0-7880-2945-5
ISBN-10: 0-7880-2945-2

ISBN-13: 978-0-7880-2944-8
ISBN-10: 0-7880-2944-4

PRINTED IN USA

Contents

Ordering Up A Set Of False Gods On Amazon

How can we thank God enough for you in return for all the joy that we feel before our God because of you? Night and day we pray most earnestly that we may see you face to face and restore whatever is lacking in your faith.

Now may our God and Father himself and our Lord Jesus direct our way to you. And may the Lord make you increase and abound in love for one another and for all, just as we abound in love for you. And may he so strengthen your hearts in holiness that you may be blameless before our God and Father at the coming of our Lord Jesus with all his saints. (1 Thessalonians 3:9-13)

As this Advent season begins, what have you promised yourself about the holidays this year? Are you vowing to have a simpler Christmas? Planning to make time for some activity you love, or time with beloved people?

What promises are ahead for your family? Do you know some kids who are waiting eagerly to see what Santa will bring? Adults who are waiting eagerly to collapse, and finally get some rest? People who find this time of year hard, and are just hoping to get through it?

This is the season when we stop and see the wealth of God's promises to us, as people of faith. We all have our own plans and promises to make and keep, but we are also swept up into God's plans at this time of year. Writing to the people of faith in the city of Thessalonica, Paul is remembering the promises that God has already kept in their lives.

The book of Acts (Chapter 17) tells us about Paul's time with the church as Thessalonica. Paul and Silas come to town and speak in the synagogue there, and tell the story of Jesus. Acts 17 says, they were "explaining and proving that it was necessary for the Messiah to suffer and to rise from the dead, and saying, 'This is the Messiah, Jesus whom I am proclaiming to you.' Some of them were persuaded and joined Paul and Silas, as did a great many of the devout Greeks and not a few of the leading women." But some of the people in town are not persuaded. In fact, they're mad. They run Paul and Silas out of town.

In this letter, Paul writes to those who believe, and he commends the believers.

They have made a dramatic change in their lives, turning away from their old religions and toward this new, uncertain, chaotic faith in Jesus. In those early days, there weren't organized churches, books, and systems of belief. Many communities met to worship in people's homes. Every area had its own practices and habits. There was no Bible, as we have one, with an agreed-upon list of books. Each area probably had their own gospel, and maybe a letter or two from Paul. They had to find their way into faith without the support of the community all around them.

It's a lot like being a Christian in our world.

Our lives are packed with idols and fake gods, too. Just like the people of Thessalonica, we're surrounded by idols. Ours come in disguise, so they're harder to avoid. Our old friend consumerism comes out in full force this time of year, and we think that the best gift will fix a relationship, or make up for our neglect all year. All year long, this particular idol tells us that the right car, the right kitchen remodel, the right outfit, or the right man cave in the basement will make our lives complete. When it never does, there's always something else to buy in the hope it will fill a hole inside us.

There are other idols and false gods, too.

There's perfectionism. If we just host the perfect party, keep a perfect house, find the perfect job, we think, then our lives will be perfect, too. Then there's the false god of busy-ness. Our culture believes that being busy is a sign that we're doing something important. There's the idol of making our kids fit our expectations, instead of living up to their own talents. There is the false god of appearances, and thinking that how we look matters.

There are plenty of idols and false gods all around us. This time of year, they call to us especially hard. The holidays ramp everything up, and we can fall into these temptations so easily. Like the early Christians in Thessalonica, we have to turn away from the idols and false gods all around us to turn toward Jesus. We have to let go of the voices all around us that are telling us to do more, buy more, go faster, and instead turn toward to voice of Jesus.

Advent invites us into a time when we determine to get ready for Jesus' coming into the world again. To get ready, we have to do the same thing — turn away from the idols of perfection, busyness, and consumerism. Advent calls us back to our faith, back to the core of who we are, and back from the false gods and idols that speak to us so alluringly.

Ron Levin tells about his own turn toward Christ in a moving memoir.

His father was born in a small Russian village, to Jewish parents. Not long afterward, his grandparents left Europe, fleeing the pogroms. In Philadelphia, his father married his high school sweetheart and tried to last through the Great Depression. The family eventually moved to North Carolina, and as the newcomers in town, he said, "we had an accent people laughed at, a name no one got right and a religion everyone got wrong." It was not easy to grow up Jewish in a small North Carolina town.

There were daily taunts and punches from the other kids in town, and the weekly attempt to keep their Jewish faith alive, with no supportive community around them. They had to drive fifty miles to the nearest synagogue for the holy days. God seemed frightening and far away. A deep loneliness settled into Ron Levin.

He longed for a closer God than the distant God he knew. He remembered, "I yearned for a God whom I could get close to, put my arms around, and cry with in the deep-sea darkness of my childhood....*God Will Punish You* was written large in our daily lives."

Neither college nor work filled the empty hole within him. He became wildly successful in his work life, and yet more lonely in his personal life. He tried all kinds of jobs, including nightclub entertainer and peach grower. He married, had a daughter, and divorced.

His friends made him promise to pray, and when he did, things happened. He was touched and blessed by the things that happened, but it was never quite enough for God to get his attention. He finally had to face the loneliness and the emptiness. All the idols of success, money, and fame were not saving him from himself.

"Why continue," he wondered, as a gun lay nearby. He managed to make a phone call to a friend, who heard his pain and urged him to open a Bible and read Romans 7 and 8. Reading the words of another Jew, something finally hit home. He slept, and in the morning he called his friend and said he wanted to be baptized. He said, "The destructive behavior patterns and hollow values that had been my idols had been sloughed off with no conscious effort on my part. It was as though a sign had been hung on me: 'Under New Management'."

He found his way to seminary, and now pastors a small country church, where he speaks about the God he has come to know well. The idols of his past life are gone, and God's promise of new life is abundantly full in his life. His days are full as he passes on the good news he knows well. He said, "Yeshua died for all, not just some of us, and I am not making a pitch: I am passing on a promise" (*The Christian Century*, January 4-11, 1995).

There is nothing that we can make, buy, order, or bake this Christmas that will make God love us any more or any less. There is a promise that has already been made and kept for us. We can turn away from the shiny false gods of our world, and turn toward the God who promises us abundant joy, through our faith. As Paul prayed for the church and for us, may God "make you increase and abound in love for one another and for all…and may God so strengthen your hearts in holiness." This is the gift that we are promised — all we have to do is claim and keep the promise.

In the name of the one who comes, Amen.

Prayer:

O God of promise, we long for your coming, with a desperate desire deeper than anything else in our lives. Turn our hearts from shiny things and our eyes from things that don't satisfy, and bring us closer to you in this Advent season. We know that you are coming to us again, and we long for the deep peace of your presence. Make us ready, we pray, so we can promise ourselves to you again. In the name of the Christ Child, Amen.

God's Evite: Wait!

On this second Sunday of Advent, we hear Paul's words to the church at Philippi, a church he knew well.

I thank my God every time I remember you, constantly praying with joy in every one of my prayers for all of you, because of your sharing in the gospel from the first day until now. I am confident of this, that the one who began a good work among you will bring it to completion by the day of Jesus Christ.

It is right for me to think this way about all of you, because you hold me in your heart, for all of you share in God's grace with me, both in my imprisonment and in the defense and confirmation of the gospel. For God is my witness, how I long for all of you with the compassion of Christ Jesus.

And this is my prayer, that your love may overflow more and more with knowledge and full insight to help you to determine what is best, so that in the day of Christ you may be pure and blameless, having produced the harvest of righteousness that comes through Jesus Christ for the glory and praise of God (Philippians 1:3-11).

Advent is, as we know, the season of waiting...but who wants a whole season devoted to waiting? We hate to wait.

In truth, we don't have to wait.

Just outside the church doors, Christmas is everywhere. There's Christmas music on. In fact, it's been on since Halloween. Christmas cards are arriving, for the people who still send cards. We're in the season of holiday parties and get-togethers with friends and family. There's a job to do every day, to get ready for Christmas.

Why bother with Advent?

Why bother to think about waiting, when we're busy already?

Oddly, God invites us to wait...practically sends us a personal invitation, with the season of Advent. God invites us to set aside the rush, the lists, the hurry, the overwhelming presence of Christmas and take a step back. God invites us to choose to wait.

Waiting is like building a muscle. The more we plan to do it, choose to do it, and commit to doing it, the better we get at it. Like woodworking, quilting, cooking, running, understanding football, or doing yoga, the more we do it, the better we get. Like all of those things, it's a skill we develop. Advent invites us to let go of the frenzy outside us, and develop our gift for waiting on God.

As Paul wrote to the Philippian church, there was a lot in his mind to remember. The book of Acts, which tells about his time in Philippi, says that he came to the city and found a group of women down by the river, working away (see Acts 16:12-40). He met Lydia and a group of others. It was the sabbath day, but he found them at the river, so we have to wonder what it was about their work was so demanding that they worked on the sabbath. Did they need the money? Their job was dyeing cloth purple. This was a labor-intensive process to produce this rare, expensive cloth.

Maybe Lydia and her co-workers thought Paul would be a diversion while they worked. He could provide some entertainment to pass the time while they worked at this tedious process. Or maybe they were annoyed. They were working and talking, and here came a stranger to interrupt with a long monologue about some guy named Jesus ... a little first-century man-splaining.

However it came about, the story says in Acts that God opened Lydia's heart to the news about Jesus.

Before he left Philippi, Paul moved on from Lydia and the women at the river. He was so overflowing with energy for God's work that he healed a slave girl, casting the demon out of her. She had a spirit that allowed her to tell people's fortunes, so once the spirit was gone, the fortunes were gone, and the money was gone. Her owners were not thrilled at her healing. They were angry because they had made so much money from her. As a result, Paul got slapped into jail in Philippi, survived an earthquake, and converted the jailer and his family to this new faith in Jesus.

All of this must have been in Paul's mind as he writes to the church in Philippi. He pictures all of these people as he wrote. Lydia and the women, with their hands stained purple from their work dyeing the cloth. The slave girl, who didn't ask to be healed, and had to find a new way to make a living. Her value didn't come from telling fortunes anymore, so what did she find to do? Did the community of believers take her in? Did she ever discover her true worth as a follower of Jesus? Paul pictures the jailer and his family, with the smaller kids now grown big, and the bigger kids on to live lives of their own.

He can see them all in his mind, as he writes.

Whose face do you see in your mind, this holiday season?

Whose face shows up as you think about the presence of God in your life? Is it the parents and grandparents who taught you this faith we have, through their actions and words? Is it the boss who saw something in you and opened a new chapter for you? How about the teacher who made you do better work? Or the partner who accepted you just as you are, setting you free to grow in new ways?

Or is it the other kind of memory that comes to mind?

Is it the people who have hurt you, and the lessons you learned from that? The people who brought you unhealed sadness, betrayal, or disappointment that you're still working on?

Or maybe there are other gifts, other people who come to mind. Think about the kids in your life who are such spiritual mirrors, reflecting back all of our flaws, as well as our gifts. Think of the faraway friends, who hold a place in your heart.

People missing from our lives make this time of year hard, too. The people who come to mind include family members lost to death. We miss them all year, but the pain is especially sharp at holiday time.

Paul wrote that he longed to see the people in Philippi who had given him so much, and there are people we long to see, too. Some will be home for the holidays, and others we won't see until we all gather around God's table someday.

With each passing year, we add more people to the gathering in our minds.

If you're a Harry Potter fan, you know that his parents died when he was a baby, but feel very present to him throughout the books. The crux of the books is Harry's battle to defeat the Lord Voldemort, who represents the forces of evil in the world. In one book, *Harry Potter and the Goblet of Fire*, Voldemort engineers it so Harry appears in a graveyard to do battle with him. Some people are bothered by the idea of witchcraft in these books, but I understand that as a literary device that allows us to see another dimension of how things happen.

In this battle in the graveyard, Harry's wand and Voldemort's wand connect. The two wands are linked to each other, spinning a golden cord between them, and out of Voldemort's wand come the people he has killed. They emerge as shadowy figures — like an echo of their former, living selves. First comes a boy who went to school with Harry, and then some other people who have been killed by Voldemort emerge. Each echo-y, shadow-y figure says something encouraging to Harry. "Hold on, Harry." "Keep going."

As he struggles to hold on, he knows who is coming next.

Finally, his parents emerge — his dad and his mom. They tell him to hold on, and then give him a piece of advice that allows him to escape. But when he needs them most, they are present with him.

The people we love and miss circle around us in the same way. They show up in our minds and we carry them in our hearts.

As we long for them, what are we to do?

Paul doesn't give us any license to lose ourselves in sorrow. He takes for granted that this longing for people will always be part of our lives, whether it's kids away at school or living their own lives, friends far away, or loved ones lost to death.

The secret to it, he says, is not hunkering down, but opening our hearts. "This is my prayer," he writes, "that your love may overflow more and more." Not that we may be safe, or free from trouble, or protected, but that our hearts are open enough to overflow with God's grace, passed on from us to others. Not that we will never know loss and sorrow, but that our hearts are wide open, to pass on God's love.

As we remember this Christmas, may we remember God's great love for us. May we slow down enough to know God's presence with us, in this season. May we become gifted at waiting, knowing that God is coming into the world again, and we want to be ready.

In the name of the Christ Child, Amen.

Prayer:
Patient God, you know we hate to wait…and yet we need to learn to stop, and watch for your presence among us. We thank you for all of the people who have brought your spirit to us, and taught faith, character and truth. Make us faithful, we pray, in waiting, and full-hearted in our rejoicing. In Jesus' name, Amen.

Joy On An Elephant

On this third Sunday of Advent, we hear again from Paul's letter to the believers at Philippi. Many scholars believe that he wrote this letter from prison, perhaps even during his last prison term in Rome, before his death, but we don't know for sure. It's clear that he wrote from a prison cell somewhere, and that he wrote about his deeply held idea of cultivating joy in all things.

Rejoice in the Lord always; again I will say, Rejoice. Let your gentleness be known to everyone. The Lord is near. Do not worry about anything, but in everything by prayer and supplication with thanksgiving let your requests be made known to God. And the peace of God, which surpasses all understanding, will guard your hearts and your minds in Christ Jesus. (Philippians 4:4-7)

In a TED Talk, Caroline Casey recalls getting the shock of her life when she was seventeen. She had plans to become a race car driver, a cowgirl, and Mowgli from "The Jungle Book." All of her dreams, she says, were about being free, having the wind in her hair and an adventure on the way. When she was seventeen, she accompanied her little sister, her visually impaired little sister to the eye doctor, just there to be a supportive big sister. This was part of their regular routine. Caroline Casey would pretend to get her eyes tested, too, as part of her support. The eye doctor knew it was her birthday, and asked what she was going to do to celebrate.

"Take a driving lesson," she told the doctor.

The eye doctor turned to her mother and said something mysterious. "You still haven't told her yet, have you?" That was the day she learned she was, and had always been, legally blind. Her parents had decided not to tell her, not to put her in a special school, not to have her live with any labels or limitations. This was their unique decision — every family makes the decision that's right for them and their kids. They wanted her to grow up, and figure out how to live in the world, on her own. For them, it was important that she be defined by her possibilities, not her limitations. As Caroline Casey says, "they gave me the ability to believe, totally, to believe that I could" (Ted Talks, August 10, 2017).

We've all had moments like her moment of shock, where despair rises up in us.

In your life, it might be a divorce, or the loss of a job. It might be losing your home or finding out that your child is in trouble. The death of a parent or sibling can knock you to your knees. Illness can shake everything up, as can the loss of a partner.

The author of this letter to the Philippians, Paul, has been knocked around himself, too. He has dealt in violence, and been beaten up and ostracized, kicked out of towns and sent on the run. But in today's reading, we hear Paul telling the church — and us — to rejoice. We overhear him telling the little church at Philippi to choose to live with joy. "Rejoice in the Lord always," he reminds them, emphasizing his point by saying it all twice.

This third Sunday in Advent is dedicated to joy. It's called the "Joy Sunday," and it's the "pink candle Sunday" on the Advent wreath. This week, we shift out of the somber tone of Advent, and turn our attention to joy.

We know Advent as a quiet season — a time of preparation for Jesus' coming. The hymns are reflective. We're supposed to be quiet and reflective. This season is supposed to create sacred space in us, so we have room for the presence of Jesus. When he's born again into our world, we want to be ready to receive him.

Unfortunately, Christmas gets in the way of Advent.

The office parties, mandatory family gatherings, shopping for gifts and groceries all create a feeling of hurry, instead of reflection. Our long lists and busy schedules to get ready for Christmas keep us from getting ready for Jesus. By this time in December, we've been hearing Christmas carols for so long that our ears are dull to them.

Rejoicing is the farthest thing from our minds.

We would happily trade rejoicing for completion. If we could only check a few things off the list, then we would rejoice.

But our faith calls us to stop and rejoice...even in Advent...even in the midst of our preparations. So, if God has placed the work, the joy, the pleasure of rejoicing at the top of our to-do lists, how do we manage it?

First, what can we jettison from our lists? What can we cross off right now, with a huge sigh of relief? What Christmas tradition is no longer giving us joy? Is there something it's time to stop doing? Is there something to move to February, when we're all bored, cranky, and need something fun to do? We have permission. God wants us to rejoice, not to be mired in things we have to do.

Second, what really makes us rejoice? Is it making something out of wood? Is it the carols? Is it the baking? Could it be getting together with college friends for a once-a-year cigar and bourbon day? Perhaps it is taking the kids to the mall to see Santa? What brings you joy at this time of year?

If we don't even know any more, if Christmas has so taken over Advent that we're not sure, we can take some wisdom from our young friends. Watch them run, full-on, toward something they're excited about. See them bouncing up and down with anticipation. Listen to how their thrilled voices get louder and louder.

What would make you feel that way this Advent? What would give you that kind of joy?

Whatever it is, God is inviting you to pursue it — this Advent, and beyond. God invites you to cultivate joy in your life, instead of distraction and hurry and worry.

Lord knows, there's plenty to get in our way.

It's not just the things we have to do.

Life itself gets in the way. We are shadowed by depression, broken by grief, frantic about paying bills, anxious about our jobs, and terrified for our kids.

And in the middle of all that, Paul tells us, as people of faith, to rejoice. Always. No matter what. He's a little nuts to ask this, but the man knows what he's talking about. Paul has been beaten and jailed, criticized and mocked, as an apostle for God. He knows something about rejoicing always.

Caroline Casey is another poster person for rejoicing always.

In her TED talk, she says that her parents, knowing that she was blind, taught her to live with a kind of dogged determination. Her father taught her how to sail, even though she couldn't see the sails or the shore, or where she was going. "But," she says, "he told me to believe and feel the wind in my face." That was enough to keep her going, and she says, "for the next eleven years, I swore nobody would ever find out that I couldn't see, because I didn't want to be a failure, and I didn't want to be weak." She chose unusual careers. She became an archaeologist, and ended up breaking lots of things. She managed a restaurant, and ended up slipping a lot.

Finally, she wore herself out. She was working for a fast-paced consulting firm, and finally had to ask for help. Admitting failure is tremendously hard. Pretending there's nothing wrong is exhausting. Being a whirlwind grows tiring, after a while.

Finally, years later, she went to see an eye specialist.

This doctor didn't bother testing her eyes. Instead, the doctor asked questions like: "Why are you fighting this so hard?" And "Do you love your job?" And "When you were little, what did you want to be?" The doctor suggested, gently, that she try something else.

Try something else? She had been trying so hard already. She crashed — emotionally, and then physically, falling in a place she knew well. In the tears and the pain, she started to think about what she had wanted to be when she was young. Being a race car driver was clearly out, but Mowgli from "The Jungle Book" was still an option. She had never been to India, didn't speak Hindi, and knew nothing about elephants, but she was determined to ride one.

"Nine months later," she says, "I had the only blind date in my life with a seven-and-a-half-foot-tall elephant called Kanchi. And together we would trek a thousand kilometers across India."

That trip turned out to raise a lot of money for cataract operations — enough for 6,000 people to see. She set up a non-profit devoted to elephant conservation. Disability, she says, is always like an elephant in the room, but it has also become a place where she feels at home. In embracing all of herself — energy, passion, and disability — she tapped into a deep, living joy within herself. On the way to her TED talk, she used her white cane, the symbol of the disability she tried to escape for so long — and guess what? It allowed her to avoid a lot of lines at the airport.

In being truly ourselves, the people God created us to be, there is the deepest joy we know. In embracing our whole lives, happiness and sorrow, grief and delight, failure and success, we come into God's presence as whole people. And there, joy is our gift, the gift that no one can rush us through, or wear out, or take away.

In the name of the joy-giver, Amen.

Prayer:
God of mystery, our lives hold sorrow and worry, and yet, underneath it all is your promise of joy, ready for us to reach out and grasp it. We thank you for leading us always toward deep joy, no matter the outer appearance of our lives. Teach us to let go of perfection, and stress, and expectation, so we can hold out our hands and receive your gift of joy. In the name of Jesus, our Redeemer, Amen.

The Gift Of — Darn It! — Waiting

On this Fourth Sunday of Advent, our season of waiting is almost over. Ready or not, Christmas is almost here. If that thought just made your heart beat faster with a feeling of stress, let's take a deep breath together and listen for God speaking.

Today's reading comes from the letters to the Hebrews, written to connect this new, early faith in Jesus back to the traditions of Judaism. The author of this book isn't known to us, but it seems to have been written to encourage believers who were facing persecution for their faith.

Consequently, when Christ came into the world, he said,
'Sacrifices and offerings you have not desired,
but a body you have prepared for me;
in burnt-offerings and sin-offerings
you have taken no pleasure.
Then I said, "See, God, I have come to do your will, O God"
(in the scroll of the book it is written of me).'
When he said above, 'You have neither desired nor taken pleasure in sacrifices and offerings and burnt-offerings and sin-offerings' (these are offered according to the law), then he added, 'See, I have come to do your will.'
He abolishes the first in order to establish the second.

And it is by God's will that we have been sanctified through the offering of the body of Jesus Christ once for all.

Over the years, I notice that my relationship with my cell phone has changed.

You may find yourself somewhere along this spectrum. At first, I had it only for emergencies. Then, I fell in love with my now-husband, and I had it for emergencies and talking to him. Then, I started to talk on it more...and my work gave me a phone that I could use for directions and reading email, which was the gateway drug to more. Some years ago, we gave up having a landline. We still have a number, so telemarketers can call us to their hearts' content, but there's no actual phone attached to it. We get a text when someone leaves us a message.

But there are flaws in this relationship of ours. I feel that the balance of power is off. Sometimes the phone drops calls, or there's an odd delay before I hear the other person, leaving us to talk over each other. Experts call this gap before we hear the other person "cell phone latency." I call it annoying.

The season of Advent in the church calendar has a similar feeling of delay and disconnection from the rest of our lives. If you've been out shopping, you know that the stores are full of Christmas carols and Santas. Decorations are everywhere, and friends and family are celebrating with festive gatherings. It's Christmas everywhere!

Except church...we're the only ones with this odd season of Advent. We're out of step. I wonder sometimes if we should just give it up and have a month of Christmas, like the rest of the world. Well, Christmas starts in September out there, but we could have the month of December as the Christmas season. We could just do away with Advent altogether. It's an odd season. We're supposed to be reflecting, but we don't have time. We're supposed to pause, but we can't seem to do it. The hymns are somber, and we'd rather sing Christmas carols all month anyway. There's never enough time for Christmas carols.

And then we have these texts. On the last Sunday in Advent, when we're inching toward Christmas, we get the book of Hebrews.

What does this have to do with Advent, anyway?

Today's text shows us another side of Jesus. As we wait for his coming, we've heard texts that understand him as the one who fulfills God's ancient promises, who changes our lives, who brings us joy. Now we have this image of Christ as our high priest — the one who intercedes for us with God, and who connects us to God.

In the Jewish tradition, the high priest was human, and was able to understand human frailty and the hopes of the people. He (always a he, in those days) was also chosen by God for this role. He stood in a unique place between God and the worshipers. You can see why early Christians picked up this image for Jesus, whom we call both human and divine. Jesus, too, stands in this distinctive place, with a unique understanding of humanity and a special understanding of God.

The early Christian faith grew out of the Jewish faith, and so this image would have been familiar to the believers. The writers of this passage took a well-known religious figure, and made it unique to our

Christian faith with the presence of Jesus. Just in case we're tempted to think too much about Jesus as a baby, or as the dusty, sweaty figure who walked all over Palestine, this text offers us another image of him. This is a figure deserving of our awe. This is a figure to make us stop and take note, not to be taken for granted. This is where we need to pause and take in the mystery of Jesus, with all of the sides and facets that we don't see during most of the Christian year.

Advent is that place where we pause and take in Jesus in a new way. We stop for surprise, and rest in awe.

This doesn't come easily, especially in this season when there's so much to do. But Advent invites us to choose to stop. We take a spiritual and mental break, and take in the wonder of the Jesus who comes as a baby, and the Christ who is our high priest, our connection to God.

Author Gretchen Rubin, who writes about happiness, says that there's hope for us. We can learn this skill of pausing. When we do, our faith grows richer. We can learn to embrace the things that are difficult. Anyone can learn to wait, gracefully…even productively. In this season, when God invites us into a time of waiting for Jesus, waiting for God's good news, we can transform our experience of waiting.

The practice of our faith is the practice of waiting, in Advent. Gretchen Rubin says we can make waiting into a fruitful activity. She suggested that we put the word "meditation" with any activity where we have to wait, any activity that's difficult for us, and let it become our teacher. It might be "cell phone delay meditation" or "waiting for school pick-up meditation" or "watching soccer practice mediation." It could even be "paying bills meditation" or "gift wrapping meditation."

Rubin adds another suggestion, *"Dig in.* As they say, if you can't get out of it, get into it." We can't get out of it Advent...so we might as well get into it, embrace it, savor it, even up to the very last day. She adds, "If something is boring for two minutes, do it for four minutes. If it's still boring, do it for eight minutes, then sixteen, and so on. Eventually, you discover that it's not boring at all" (from her blog, GretchenRubin.com). If we're not good at waiting, the cure, it turns out, is to do more waiting. If we find something annoying, the solution is to embrace it.

Advent makes that come alive in our faith.

Advent calls us out of the rush, the hurry, the overwhelming madness of Christmas, into a stillness where we meet Jesus the high priest. We learn to pause and then learn *from* the pause. Advent invites us to stop, to wait, to dig in, and to find the mysterious presence of Jesus again as we do. It makes us suspend the world's time, and get on God's time.

And that is our very best preparation for Christmas.

In the name of the Christ Child, Amen.

Prayer:
Merciful God, save us, we pray, from rushing through these days. Stop our hurrying so we breathe deeply of your presence. Still our busy fingers so they can fold in prayer. Slow our rushing steps, so we see you in one another's faces. Make us wait, we pray, so we can take in the fullness of your Presence, as you come to us again in Jesus. Amen.

The Best Gifts

Our Christmas Eve reading takes a different turn this year, as we read from the letter to Titus. This is one of the shortest books in the Bible, and is almost never read in worship. But the writer has an unusual take on the gifts of Christmas.

For the grace of God has appeared, bringing salvation to all, training us to renounce impiety and worldly passions, and in the present age to live lives that are self-controlled, upright, and godly, while we wait for the blessed hope and the manifestation of the glory of our great God and Savior, Jesus Christ. He it is who gave himself for us that he might redeem us from all iniquity and purify for himself a people of his own who are zealous for good deeds. (Titus 2:11-14)

You might be wondering why in the world someone would choose to read a scripture from Titus on Christmas Eve. You might even be feeling a little — or a lot — cheated — right now. You came to church on this special night expecting the familiar story of a baby in a manger, angels announcing good news into the night sky and stunned but willing shepherds going to take a look. That's the Christmas story, right? Not this puzzling text from Titus. This is a really unexpected reading for Christmas Eve.

But Titus tells a different version of the Christmas story. He tells about what happened after Jesus was born, and lives and dies.

We don't know much about Titus. In a way, he's a stand-in for you, or for me. He is a kind of blank slate. His faith is a stand-in for ours, too. Titus probably came to faith through Paul's teaching, or through someone like Paul. The writer called Titus "my true child in a common faith" (1:4). Another scripture tells us that Titus accompanied Paul on his third missionary journey, and visited the churches in Corinth at least once. Paul had a lot of affection for Titus, but we don't know much more about him. The letter lives on not because of Titus himself, but because the author has a sense of an unexpected gift — something startling that has come into the world.

The author is full of awe at how the world has changed because of the life of Jesus Christ. God has changed the world, and so people are called to live in a different kind of way. When our lives change, the gift of Jesus lives on. It gets passed on from person to person, through the years.

In this amazing gift of Jesus, the lost are redeemed. The hopeless have hope. The struggling find a way to live in God's light. These are the gifts of Christmas.

The story is told (by author Brian Joseph) about a five-year-old boy who unwrapped his gifts of Christmas morning. His mother let him play with them for a while, and then asked which one he would like to give away to a poorer child who needed a gift.

"None of them," the boy told her.

The mother sat down with him and explained that the power of a gift was in its sharing. Helping other people was an important part of the holiday spirit.

This was a hard sell, but the boy agreed to share one of his gifts. His mother let him think about it until the next day.

This was a hard choice. There was a book, a toy flute, a Popeye book bag, and a toy dump truck with doors that opened. Finally, he chose the flute, and he and his mother took it to the Salvation Army, where they would make sure it got to a child who could use it. "How will they know it is for a child?" the boy asked his mother. She told him he would write a note and tape it to the gift. His note said: "Please be sure to give this to a kid who doesn't have a lot of toys."

The next year they did the same thing, and then the next. It became a familiar part of their Christmas tradition. Some years, the decision was really hard. The year that he anguished over the gifts, and finally decided to give up a game of checkers, his mother came in later with a piece of cardboard and some bottle caps. They made a new checkers game out of those, and played on that all year.

One year, his mother was out of work for part of the year, and there wasn't much money for gifts. His mother told him that he didn't have to give a gift away that year. He was excited at first, and then he told his mother that he wanted to give a gift away. He put his new football in the Salvation Army box.

When he grew up, he talked to his mother about this tradition, and how it seemed strange that he had to give a gift away, since they were so poor themselves. His mother just looked at him as if he hadn't learned much over the years.

After some years passed, he became a dad himself, and his own son was now five. His son asked him what had been his favorite gift when he was a child. By now, he had learned a few things, but he still struggled to explain to his young son that his best gifts never came in a box. He told his son about the childhood tradition, and his son asked if he still did that. Yes, he said, he had done it every Christmas for over thirty years. The next day, the dad chose a new sweater, wrote a note on the box, and got ready to deliver it. As he was heading out the door, his young son asked if he could come, too. The father waited in the car for his son to get ready, wondering what in the world was taking so long. Finally the little boy came out the door, holding his new playdough set.

"Dad," he asked, "can you help me write a note?" (Found on *www.katinkahesselink.net.*)

Is there a gift you can use this Christmas? Not a coffeemaker, a sweater, or a game, but a deeper gift? Has this past year held some sorrows for you? Are you looking for a gift of peace? Understanding?

Some of you lost loved ones this year, and you're wondering how you're going to make it through Christmas. Some of you separated from a partner, and are feeling the loss keenly. Some of you faced serious illness. Some of you have health concerns, and are praying for your health to be restored. Some of you have loved ones who won't be here next Christmas, and you're savoring their presence this Christmas, in all its bittersweet-ness.

For all of those things, God offers us the gift of hope, through the life-changing, world-transforming, soul-lifting gift of Jesus. This is the season of gifts, but our biggest and brightest and best gift is found in a manger, not under a tree or at a store. That is our gift in the birth of Jesus.

For that stunning gift, ready to be opened, ready to be given away, thanks be to God. Amen.

Prayer:
Generous God, may each gift we give or receive this season point us toward you, and toward the gift that that transcends all the others. In your transforming gift of hope, we know the purpose of Christmas, and for our lives. In every place of hurt, sorrow or despair, may we be open to the deep gift you give us, the promise of hope that turns everything else inside out. In Jesus' name, Amen.

First Sunday after Christmas Day
Colossians 3:12-17

If God Made New Year's Resolutions

As the calendar year draws to a close, let us listen to God's words of wisdom for the end of one year, and the start of the next.

As God's chosen ones, holy and beloved, clothe yourselves with compassion, kindness, humility, meekness, and patience. Bear with one another and, if anyone has a complaint against another, forgive each other; just as the Lord has forgiven you, so you also must forgive. Above all, clothe yourselves with love, which binds everything together in perfect harmony. And let the peace of Christ rule in your hearts, to which indeed you were called in the one body. And be thankful. Let the word of Christ dwell in you richly; teach and admonish one another in all wisdom; and with gratitude in your hearts sing psalms, hymns, and spiritual songs to God. And whatever you do, in word or deed, do everything in the name of the Lord Jesus, giving thanks to God the Father through him. (Colossians 3:12-17)

As we move from Christmas to the New Year, some of you are pondering resolutions. Is this the year to get all A's in school, or to save more money? Could we manage to lose ten pounds, or eat more kale and less dessert?

Others of you never make resolutions. Some of you are close to perfect already, and others of you don't see any hope of change.

In the middle of all those decisions, everyone has advice about making and keeping your resolutions, including one list of suggestions just for twenty-somethings. My favorite: "Wait thirty seconds before you look up a fact you can't remember on your phone, and try to remember it using your brain. This is what the olden days were like." If you're still stumped, a blogger offers a New Year's Resolution Generator. Click the button, and the site offers helpful suggestions. "Have a garage sale." "Learn Italian." "Talk more, tweet less."

Or, there's a simpler way. This passage from Colossians offers us the timeless wisdom of our faith. The author reminds us that, as followers of Jesus Christ, we have been changed already. It's not that we're going to change — although we may — but that God has already changed us into new people. Our resolutions begin with our own desires and hopes — things we want.

In the life of the spirit, though, change begins with God. Before anything else, we are chosen by God. Because of God's choice, something has already changed in us. We are already holy and special. Because of that, our choices don't belong only to us.

The great storyteller — and doctor — Rachel Naomi Remen tells a story on her blog about a trip her parents took her on when she was 11 (RachelRemen.com). She had never left New York City before, so everything was thrilling to her. She loved all of the antique shops and thrift stores they went to, and could spend hours poking through old and broken things. Everything was interesting, and worth looking at.

In one place, she saw a box marked "Free" by the cash register. She poked through the buttons, broken watches, a ring with no stone, and finally pulled out two links from an old bracelet. Her dad just laughed. "It's broken," he cautioned her. "What do you need them for?"

She felt stupid about her choice. Silly. She thought they were beautiful. But she kept them anyway, in her jewelry box. Her mother smiled and reassured her. "Someday you may discover what they're for. In the meantime they will be a nice keepsake of our trip."

The two broken bracelet pieces stayed in her drawer for years, until she was moving to California. When she found them again, she says, she finally saw their true value. She glued an earring back to each one, and still wears them as earrings. People stop her on the streets and at the store and ask where she got them. They are one of a kind, and for her they are perfect.

She says, "Things are often not what they seem. Labeling things "broken" or "useless" can keep us from seeing their true value." Everything finds its place — including us. We find where we're meant to be, and learn to see our own unique purpose.

If God made New Year's resolutions, they would be all about us: Getting us to live into our faith, leading us toward deeper faith, getting us to use our talents, instead of hiding them away, helping us find our true purpose in life. Maybe God would vow to do more smiting this year...but I doubt it.

Our lives are the vehicle for God's New Year's resolutions.

In response to God, we are to live like changed people — to put on new life like we would new clothes, letting the outside reflect the inside. We are to get our compassion, kindness, and humility out of the drawer, and wear them. We are to put on meekness and patience as the garb of our new lives. Forgiveness is required of us, not because we're super-spiritual, but because Christ has forgiven us.

This New Year and always, "As God's chosen ones, holy and beloved, clothe yourselves with compassion, kindness, humility, meekness, and patience. Bear with one another...above all, clothe yourselves with love, which binds everything together in perfect harmony... let the peace of Christ rule in your hearts...let the word of Christ dwell in you richly."

For the spirit of Christmas, and looking forward to the blessings of the New Year, thanks be to God. Amen.

Prayer:
God who longs for us to live fully, we praise you for the gifts of compassion and humility, kindness and patience, which we put on in your name. Help us to live into our true selves as we follow you. In Jesus' name, Amen.

Unusual Gifts

(Permission to use her blog post granted by Rachel Macy Stafford.)

This week we celebrate Epiphany, which is the end of the Christmas season. Epiphany is the day in the church calendar that the magi, the wise men, are celebrated. This year our reading comes from the Letter to the Ephesians, looking at Epiphany in a different way. Listen for God speaking.

This is the reason that I Paul am a prisoner for Christ Jesus for the sake of you Gentiles— for surely you have already heard of the commission of God's grace that was given to me for you, and how the mystery was made known to me by revelation, as I wrote above in a few words, a reading of which will enable you to perceive my understanding of the mystery of Christ. In former generations this mystery was not made known to humankind, as it has now been revealed to his holy apostles and prophets by the Spirit: that is, the Gentiles have become fellow-heirs, members of the same body, and sharers in the promise in Christ Jesus through the gospel.

Of this gospel I have become a servant according to the gift of God's grace that was given to me by the working of his power. Although I am the very least of all the saints, this grace was given to me to bring to the Gentiles the news of the boundless riches of Christ, and to make everyone see what is the plan of the mystery hidden for ages in God who created all things; so that through the church the wisdom of God in its rich variety might now be made known to the rulers and authorities in the heavenly places. This was in accordance with the eternal purpose that he has carried out in Christ Jesus our Lord, in whom we have access to God in boldness and confidence through faith in him.

Epiphany is the twelfth day of Christmas, which means...what? It means twelve drummers drumming, if we follow the old Christmas carol. Gosh, I hope not... after the Christmas season, I was hoping for something a little quieter. For some people, this is the day to take the tree down. Maybe you're determined to finish your returns or at least get the darn lights down?

On Epiphany we remember the arrival of the magi, or the wise men, to worship the new baby Jesus. This is a little bit of fast-forwarding in the Jesus story, like when you zoom through the commercials so you can get back to watching the show you've gotten excited about. The Bible tells us that the magi arrived when Jesus was about two years old, but the church calendar condenses that into our twelve days of Christmas.

The magi were an odd bunch. On Christmas cards, and in nativity sets, they look pretty respectable. We usually imagine that there are three of them, although the story doesn't say. But, really, this is a rather scruffy group. The first people to come and see Jesus were the smelly, disreputable shepherds, and now this crew isn't much better. Magi were interpreters of dreams. The term can also mean fortune-tellers and watchers of the stars. They're like the psychic hotline or tarot card readers of our time.

The magi are clearly foreigners. They were so clueless about where Jesus might be that they head for the court of Herod to ask where the king of the Jews has been born, assuming that a birth so momentous must be at court. Herod, who considers himself to be the king of the Jews, is not pleased with the question.

We celebrate the magi because they understand the power of the gift in Jesus' birth. They come with their own gifts to honor this child who will play such an important role in the world. "Epiphany" means "to appear" or "to make known." God is made known — not just to faithful Jews — but also to foreigners.

The writer of Ephesians also sees the gift in Jesus' birth. The world is transformed by Jesus' life among us, and by the contagious influence of his connection with God. The writer is emphatic that this gift isn't just for faithful Jewish people, but also for the Gentiles, the people who were once strangers. In a beautiful phrase, the writer says that God's wisdom has a "rich variety" and so does God's revelation to humankind. Working hard to explain this, the writer uses the word "mystery" over and over in this passage.

Now the writer is a servant of the gospel, he says, bound to pass this gift on. He, too, is an unlikely recipient of this epiphany, of this revelation. If the writer is Paul, he was formerly a persecutor of the people who followed Jesus. Now he's an advocate, a messenger for the message he once despised.

God's epiphanies don't follow the usual patterns. They go in unusual directions, to unusual people, in unusual ways.

Blogger Rachel Macy Stafford (author of the blog *Hands-Free Mama*) said that her daughter understands the importance of gifts. She has a talent for giving gifts. "Like most children, her offerings consisted of items that adults wouldn't ordinarily classify as gifts. Broken seashells, traumatized frogs, dying weeds, and misshapen rocks were often presented in small, dirt-laden hands beneath a wide smile."

Lately, her daughter has been re-gifting things she finds at home. She wraps slightly used items and passes them on, to her mother's embarrassment.

Over the years, Stafford said she has learned from her daughter about the power of the right gift. "I must be honest; I used to cringe at the sight of my child tearing through our (multiple) junk drawers looking for the perfect gift. When she found it, she would beam at the "treasure" as if she just knew the recipient was going to love it." The mother was anxious about how these gifts would be received.

She added, "Last Christmas, my daughter spent hours wrapping barely-used bottles of lotion, tiny hotel shampoos, and gently-used books. She then declared she wanted to distribute the colorful packages to homeless people in the downtown area on Christmas Eve. Her very first recipient was a frail, elderly woman with sad eyes who clutched her life possessions in a ripped trash bag. It wasn't until I watched this woman's be face completely transformed by the mere sight my pint-sized-gift-bearer that I got over myself."

In the spirit of the magi, sometimes the gift is more about our presence than something inside a box. Macy adds another story: "My daughter's best friend became suddenly ill with the flu. Within minutes of hearing the news, a card was made by my daughter and a bracelet from her drawer was lovingly wrapped. Briefly relapsing into my old ways, I felt slightly relieved that the price tag was still on the bracelet. But I was quickly reminded that the price tag meant nothing. The next day, the child's mother told me how much my daughter's gift meant to her daughter. And when the mother recounted what her child said, I could not hold back my tears.

With sincerity her daughter said: "I bet a lot of people heard I was sick. And after they said, 'That's too bad,' they just went on with their life — but not Natalie. She stopped what she was doing to show me she cared about me. She is the best friend anyone could have." Macy notes that "our most precious gift is when we stop in the midst of our busy lives and give a piece of ourselves ... our attention, a listening ear, a lingering embrace, a word of encouragement, meaningful eye contact, snuggles in bed, one-on-one time, or a helping hand. In order to give our most precious commodity — the gift of ourselves — we must let go of all that distracts us from what truly matters. Perhaps the perfect gift is not in the getting, but rather in the letting go."

In Jesus, we all receive a gift. Epiphany speaks again of the power of this gift — revealed to travelers, and strangers, to fortune tellers and unlikely people. It's revealed to those unlikely people, and revealed again by them. We know on Epiphany that gifts are contagious. Like the writer of Ephesians, we can't keep them to ourselves. We have to give them away.

The magi also have a gift to share with us. They speak to us through the ages of the power of persistence — they don't give up when they get to Jerusalem, and there's no baby there. They're willing to travel on to a really improbable place. God shows up, not at the court and not at the temple, but in a shabby room in a little town. They may be fortune tellers, but the magi are wise enough to know that they're seeing the real thing — and they fall to their knees.

May we, too, see God's gifts, and pass them on. In Jesus' name, Amen.

Prayer:
God of such generosity, make us alert, we pray, to your appearing, to the places you choose to make yourself known to us. Help us to see your gifts, to follow them where they lead, and to pass them on with a generosity that echoes yours. In the name of our best gift, Jesus, Amen.

The Holy Spirit Brings Everyone To The Party

On this Sunday after Epiphany, we celebrate Jesus' baptism, and the gift of the Holy Spirit that comes to him that day. The reading for today looks at the same gift — the coming of the Holy Spirit — to a community of believers.

Listen for God speaking:

Now when the apostles at Jerusalem heard that Samaria had accepted the word of God, they sent Peter and John to them. The two went down and prayed for them that they might receive the Holy Spirit (for as yet the Spirit had not come upon any of them; they had only been baptized in the name of the Lord Jesus). Then Peter and John laid their hands on them, and they received the Holy Spirit. (Acts 8:14-17)

One of the things I love in life is the advice column. It comes in a lot of forms, from the original — Dear Abby — to lots of modern, sassier forms. If you need advice on anything in the world, you can write to Dear Amy, who is Dear Abby's successor, or Dear Prudence, or even get on the Dear Sugars podcast. I love to read the question, or listen to it, and think about what I might suggest, and then to hear the wise answer that comes. I love to hear what the experts think of that I miss, or see where I disagree with their advice.

Today's scripture reads like a request for advice. The new believers need help from people more established in faith. We can imagine these new converts in Samaria writing to the established church in Jerusalem for advice, when they find something lacking in their new faith.

Dear Peter and the faithful in Jerusalem:

We have heard about your faith, and the amazing gift of the Holy Spirit that came upon all of you at Pentecost. We all know the story of Pentecost, and how you waited in Jerusalem, just the way Jesus told you to, for the blessing of the Holy Spirit. Then on Pentecost, the Spirit came in a way that you couldn't miss. A rush of wind. Tongues of fire. The ability to speak so all those travelers in Jerusalem heard you in their own languages.

We have been baptized, but we haven't experienced anything like that. Is it possible that the Holy Spirit hasn't come to us yet? Are we doing something wrong? Is there something wrong with our faith? Should we do something different to get the Holy Spirit to come?

Sincerely,

Baptized but Spiritless in Samaria

Somehow, Peter and the crew in Jerusalem learned that there were people who wanted to follow the way of Christ. They have been baptized, but these new believers are lacking the fire and energy and mystery that the Spirit brings. Peter and John decide to head out to help them with this problem.

The Samaritan people have come to faith in Jesus through Philip, who is out on a road trip, preaching and teaching people about Jesus. The book of Acts (Acts 8:5-13) tells us that it starts out this way:

> *Philip went down to the city of Samaria and proclaimed the Messiah to them. The crowds with one accord listened eagerly to what was said by Philip, hearing and seeing the signs that he did, for unclean spirits, crying with loud shrieks, came out of many who were possessed; and many others who were paralyzed or lame were cured. So there was great joy in that city...But when they believed Philip, who was proclaiming the good news about the kingdom of God and the name of Jesus Christ, they were baptized, both men and women.*

You remember the Samaritans.

Those were the people the Jews hated. The two groups were close cousins, different branches that grew out of the same Jewish faith and went in different directions. Over the years, hatred grew up between them. Each group looked down on the other, and the two groups went in different directions in their faith.

You remember that Jesus traveling around in Gentile territory was shocking to people. People wondered how Jesus could be a learned rabbi and not know how awful these people were. The story of the Good Samaritan was upsetting to people because no one believed a Samaritan could be good. When Jesus met the woman at the well in Samaria, the disciples wondered why he was even talking to her. Jesus himself told a Samaritan woman, who asked for her daughter to be healed, that it was not fair to take the children's food and throw it to the dogs.

There's a lot of history — and a lot of hatred — in that.

Now these people have come to faith in Jesus.

Peter and John headed out to check it out. Maybe they're amazed…or thrilled…or suspicious. The story doesn't say. Whatever they talked about, whatever worries they had as they traveled, whatever they thought while they were on the way, by the time they got there, Peter and John were ready. They prayed for those new believers that they would receive the Holy Spirit — the same gift given to Jesus at his own baptism. The Spirit continued to move into these new believers, in the same way that it came to Jesus, and to Peter and John, and to the other followers of Jesus.

This gift, given to Jesus in the Jordan River, continued to move among the followers of Jesus. It continues to live in each of us, and in our community when we gather.

The story of the early church is a story of conversions. Someone unlikely is converted into faith: a eunuch, a Samaritan, a Roman soldier. But the conversion always goes both ways. The follower of Jesus learns something from the other person, too. Here Peter and John are moved out of their traditional hatred for the Samaritans, moved to pray for them, moved to rejoice when the Holy Spirit came.

Perhaps you heard the story last year about the American soldier from World War Two who was determined to return a flag to Japan.

Japanese soldiers in World War Two carried flags called "good luck flags." Friends and family signed the white spaces of the flags, and then gave the flag to a soldier who was leaving for war. The soldier carried the personalized flag as a precious memento of home. In the Battle of Saipan, then-Marine Marvin Strombo got separated from his unit, and found himself behind enemy lines. He saw the flag and took it from the body a Japanese soldier who had been killed in the battle. The flag came home with him after the war. These flags were prized keepsakes among American soldiers in the dramatic, difficult days of World War Two.

Strombo said he felt bad taking the flag originally, and was determined to return it. According to NPR, "Strombo had long desired to return [the flag]...It wasn't until he visited a Japanese culture class at the University of Montana last year that Strombo learned what the Japanese writing on the flag was and what the flags meant to the families of the fallen" (NPR.org).

Now in his nineties, Marvin Strombo didn't know how much time he would have, so he contacted the Obon Society. The Obon Society has a mission of promoting peace by returning flags and personal artifacts to Japan. As the Greatest Generation comes to the end of their lives, there is a lot of memorabilia that former soldiers, or their families, want to see returned (ObonSociety.org).

Reading the calligraphy on the flag, the Obon Society narrowed the search down to a region, and then a village, and then a family. They determined that the flag belonged to Lance Corporal Yasue. Yasue had left home in 1943, died in battle, and his remains were never repatriated. His family received a coffin full of stones.

Strombo traveled to the small village in Japan where Yasue's family still lived, and presented the flag to Yasue's younger brother, now 89 and still working the family farm. Yasue's family was grateful to receive the flag as a remembrance of the brother who never returned home. At that moment, Marvin Strombo and the Yasue family weren't enemies divided by war, but people who shared a common experience of pain and loss.

The gift of the Holy Spirit does the same thing.

It leaps across every dividing line we can think of. It heals old divisions, and brings peace to old hurts. It reveals that we are all equal in God's sight. It makes the Samaritan believers as good as the Jewish believers. It makes people who come later just as good as the people who start out in faith. It draws us all toward Jesus, and erases the lines we draw between ourselves.

The Holy Spirit enfolds us all into God's plans.

It brings us all into God's community. The Holy Spirit links us back to Jesus and his baptism, and it moves us to follow him into the work God has for us to do.

May we be watching for signs of the Spirit, and go where it leads us, following Jesus. In his name, Amen.

Prayer:
God of mysterious grace, we thank you for the gift of your Holy Spirit. We praise you that you continue to touch us with your Spirit, knocking down our walls, giving energy to our faith, leading us toward you. We pray that you would nurture the gift of the Spirit within us and within all people, breaking down all that divides us. Make our faith greater than all of the world's obstacles, we pray. In your holy name, Amen.

The Limping Body Of Christ

We continue, this week, and for the next few weeks in the season of Epiphany. This is the season of light. In these dark winter days, the Christian calendar gives us a whole season of light. The theme of this season is the way God is made known to humanity. You'll see those themes of light and revelation all through the readings in this Epiphany season.

Today's reading comes from Paul's letter to the church in the city of Corinth. The believers in Corinth are trying to figure out how to live together in within the bounds of their new faith in Jesus.

Now concerning spiritual gifts, brothers and sisters, I do not want you to be uninformed. You know that when you were pagans, you were enticed and led astray to idols that could not speak. Therefore I want you to understand that no one speaking by the Spirit of God ever says 'Let Jesus be cursed!' and no one can say 'Jesus is Lord' except by the Holy Spirit.

Now there are varieties of gifts, but the same Spirit; and there are varieties of services, but the same Lord; and there are varieties of activities, but it is the same God who activates all of them in everyone. To each is given the manifestation of the Spirit for the common good. To one is given through the Spirit the utterance of wisdom,

and to another the utterance of knowledge according to the same Spirit, to another faith by the same Spirit, to another gifts of healing by the one Spirit, to another the working of miracles, to another prophecy, to another the discernment of spirits, to another various kinds of tongues, to another the interpretation of tongues. All these are activated by one and the same Spirit, who allots to each one individually just as the Spirit chooses.
(1 Corinthians 12:1-11)

Have you been to that family gathering, the one where everything starts off well? Things are going fine. No one has asked you when you're going to get married, or have a baby, or get a real job. No one is drinking too much just yet, and the conversation is still polite. The uncle who likes to stir things up hasn't brought up politics yet, and no one is criticizing anyone's kids. Yet.

Somehow, the feeling that it's going to fall apart is in the air.

That's how family meals seemed to go for the early church in Corinth. The disagreements were so pointed that they wrote to Paul with some specific questions, and he attempted to answer them in this letter.

Like many churches, the church in Corinth was a curious mixture of people who had nothing in common. Some were owners of slaves, and some were slaves ... wealthy people, and then day laborers, worried about working to eat ... merchants, and artisans. There were busy households, and single people. There were older people, honoring the old traditions, and young people, wanting something new.

Coming from such different backgrounds, it was hard to understand each other. The fights were inevitable. Paul wrote at least two long letters to the church at Corinth, and probably more, trying to answer all the questions they raised. He answered what to do about women ... the proper way to celebrate the Lord's Supper ... whose gifts were better and more valuable for the church. The original questions have been lost, but we have Paul's answers. A lot of what he wrote is practical advice, but here he has a vision of the Christian community as a place where all of the members lean on each other, and benefit from each other's gifts.

It seems simple enough. The community needs everyone's talents and experiences, or they will be one-sided. He tells them that the lawyers needed to appreciate the artists, and the engineers need to listen to the poets, the extroverts need to wait for the introverts to catch up, the people with disabilities need to teach the rest of us, the athletes need to slow down for the people with walkers, and the teachers need to appreciate the musicians. Paul was addressing the whole community of the church in this passage. It isn't meant for a few individuals in their faith lives, but for the whole community.

But in real life, the engineers wanted the poets to think like engineers. The cooks wanted everyone to sit down and eat together, and the math wizards couldn't be bothered with food. The extroverts thought the introverts should just speak up and say what's on their minds, and the introverts wished the extroverts would just shut up.

Into the midst of these bitter feelings and flying words, Paul sends this letter, trying to make peace. He wrote to this one congregation, but his letter applies to every congregation I've ever known. He's talking about how the people of God are to treat each other when they have differences — handy advice for every church. A church without differences is a cult. This passage is so familiar that we read it without hearing it, but there's news here for us, too.

The strange and uncomfortable news is that our differences come from God. The person you've been trying to win over to your way of thinking — a gift from God. The person who drives you crazy because she's so creative, but can never get organized...the person who's so organized that you feel like he's a drill sergeant, but everything runs smoothly when he's around...the guy who you think is a flake, but he's great with the youth group...the person who notices every detail when you like to see the big picture, or vice versa. All of these people are gifts from God.

We often think that life would be so much better if other people would get it together — meaning: if they would just think like we do. If we just thought alike, then surely the business of the church would go so much more smoothly. But here Paul is telling us that those differences are God's blessings.

Your gift of teaching...and yours of ushering, welcoming guests with a huge, friendly smile...and yours, of planning programs, and yours, of working with kids...your gifts of money, and time, and ideas, and plans to make things better...are all important. If anyone decides to stay home, there's a hole in the fabric, an empty place at the table. It is better to have disagreements at the table than empty places.

It all sounds good, but how do we live with people so different from us, without arguing and poking at each other? How do we make sense of the people who bewilder us?

In a recent interview featured on OnBeing.org, civil rights icon Ruby Sales said there's one question we can ask each other that always works. Ruby Sales is highlighted in the new Museum of African-American History, and she runs the non-profit Spirit House Project in Atlanta. She grew up in the segregated South, where injustice ran deep, and there were huge divides between people.

The first time she went to a civil rights demonstration, she said, "we were surrounded by horses and state troopers who wouldn't let us go to the bathroom, and I kept looking up at the sky, waiting for the Exodus story to happen to me...I expected God to appear and some chariot to open up in the sky, because I couldn't imagine that we were so right, and God would be so wrong." But God didn't show up as she imagined God would.

The question she learned from that, the one that always works, is: "Where does it hurt?" We each carry different beliefs and live with different struggles. This question allows us to see each other. We get past the aggravations and move toward understanding.

Once we understand each other, our differences are illuminating. They teach us and enlarge us. I notice that the person who aggravates me most in any situation often turns out to be the one I can learn the most from. The person who's so different from me that I wonder where in the world they got those ideas ends up teaching me something -- if I can take a deep breath, and really listen. We think differences are something to overcome, but they are the meeting ground of the Spirit.

You may think the church doesn't need your time — that someone else can do what you do. You may think that the church doesn't need your money — that it's too small to matter, or too unimportant. You may think the church doesn't need your ideas — but you might be the only one who sees it the way you do.

Families can be hard, and the church is no different.

A friend of mine and her adult sister fought for two decades about something that seemed important when it began. When their mother died, they discovered that they needed each other to grieve and remember their mom. "My sister and I are speaking," she told me one day. "It's so great that we could do this, put aside our arguments…and, of course, my mother prayed for this every day for twenty years."

The hanging in, the daily work, joins us together in the end.

So, how do we live together as a church community? As a denomination?

Paul says…we don't have to *make* ourselves into one body.

He is saying that God has *already* made us into one body … like it or not. Now we must live as if we believe it, because we are *already* bound together, made one, fed at one table.

The promise of God's making us into one body is that our divisions, our arguments, our fights are not the last word. There is something bigger. The body may limp along or be broken at times but it is still there. The Spirit never intends for us all to be the same…but to live together, work together, serve together, look into the future together, worship together…and belong together.

That's the family we can be. That's the community that's worthy of our gifts. Amen.

Prayer:

God of surprising gifts, we thank you for the gifts in one another, the ones we value and the ones we don't understand, the ones we admire and the ones we can't stand. Weave us together, we pray, into a rich and diverse community, living as members of a common body, enlivened by Jesus. We give you our thanks, and pray in Jesus' name. Amen.

Nose Hairs And Disney

We continue listening to Paul's letter to the early Christians in the city of Corinth. In this reading, he continues with his vision of the church as a body with many, equally important members.

For just as the body is one and has many members, and all the members of the body, though many, are one body, so it is with Christ. For in the one Spirit we were all baptized into one body — Jews or Greeks, slaves or free — and we were all made to drink of one Spirit.

Indeed, the body does not consist of one member but of many. If the foot were to say, 'Because I am not a hand, I do not belong to the body', that would not make it any less a part of the body. And if the ear were to say, 'Because I am not an eye, I do not belong to the body', that would not make it any less a part of the body. If the whole body were an eye, where would the hearing be? If the whole body were hearing, where would the sense of smell be? But as it is, God arranged the members in the body, each one of them, as he chose. If all were a single member, where would the body be? As it is, there are many members, yet one body. The eye cannot say to the hand, 'I have no need of you', nor again the head to the feet, 'I have no need of you.' On the contrary, the members of the body that seem to be weaker are indispensable, and those members of the body that we think less honorable we clothe with greater honor, and our less respectable members are treated with greater respect; whereas our more respectable members do not need this. But God has so arranged the body, giving the greater honor to the inferior member, that there may be no dissension within the body, but the members may have the same care for one another. If one member suffers, all suffer together with it; if one member is honored, all rejoice together with it.

Now you are the body of Christ and individually members of it. And God has appointed in the church first apostles, second prophets, third teachers; then deeds of power, then gifts of healing, forms of assistance, forms of leadership, various kinds of tongues. Are all apostles? Are all prophets? Are all teachers? Do all work miracles? Do all possess gifts of healing? Do all speak in tongues? Do all interpret? But strive for the greater gifts. And I will show you a still more excellent way. (1 Corinthians 12:12-31a)

Did you have field day at school when you were growing up?

Depending on your level of athletic talent, field day could be a thrilling escape from school or an exercise in torture. If you had some outdoor skills, field day was a diversion from the classroom at the end of the school year. It was hot and everyone was bored. You got to go outside and finally show the A-plus math students what real talent was. Or, if you had zero athletic skills, it was just a long hot day of torture in the sun, when you'd rather be reading a book.

Love it or hate it, a staple of field day was the three-legged race, where two people — with four legs — had to work together to race on three legs. There's a lot of lurching and stumbling.

This is the image that comes to mind when Paul talks about the church as one body. It's a body like Mr. Potato Head, with all kinds of ill-fitting parts, stumbling along as if on three uncoordinated legs.

But, coordinated or not, good-looking or not, Paul says that all of us who follow Christ are all part of one body.

In last week's reading, Paul made a case for the diversity of the church, and the way we need each other's gifts. The thinkers need the do-ers, and the action people need the prayer warriors. To have a church be complete, we need ushers, bookkeepers, and quiet listeners. We need planners and people who are peaceful to be with. We need older people with wisdom and younger people with a different view of the world. All of us, together, make the church richer.

There's a place for each part of the body. One writer, Brian Volck, of *The Ekklesia Project* said that his wife once lamented how little she seemed to be doing in life. Other people were learning languages, saving children from human trafficking, starting non-profits, attending law school, and she felt like her life just didn't measure up. A friend considered what she said, and then answered, "All those things are important, but we're all part of the body of Christ, and we have a role, however small. So what if you're the nose hair? You're there for a purpose. You may not have any idea what good you're doing, but that's still your job: to be a nose hair in the body of Christ."

I can't tell if that's reassuring, or not.

Once we understand that we are all parts of the same body, the question becomes how we treat each other. He moves beyond tolerance here, and calls us to the work of being compassionate to each other. Each one of us is a member of this same body, and we are meant to see each other with compassion.

In their book *Proof*, Daniel Montgomery and Timothy Paul Jones tell the story of Timothy's daughter. She had been adopted by another family previously, had a couple of rough years with that family and then the adoption was dissolved. She never quite became part of the first family, which left her with a deep sense of mistrust. At the age of eight, she was adopted by Timothy and his family.

Whenever the first adoptive family went to Disney World, they took their biological children, but left this little girl behind. She was left feeling like she had always done something wrong and couldn't be included in the trip. By the time she came to her new family, she had seen tons of pictures of Disney, and had heard all about it, but was never included in a trip, so he made plans to take the whole family, including their new daughter.

But the very idea of the trip kicked up something in this little girl. Her behavior got worse and worse. She lied, stole food that they would have given her, whispered cruel things to her sisters, and it all got worse as the trip approached. Timothy said that a few days before the trip, he settled his newest daughter on his lap to ask what was going on. "I know what you're going to do," she said. "You're not going to take me to Disney World, are you?"

It was tempting — really tempting.

Suddenly, her awful behavior made sense. "She knew she couldn't earn her way into the Magic Kingdom — she had tried and failed that test several times before." So she was going in the opposite direction instead.

He asked her: "Is this trip something we're doing as a family?" She nodded. "Are you part of this family?" Another nod. "Then you're going with us... you're part of our family, and we're not leaving you behind."

Her behavior still grew worse until it was time to leave for the trip, but they were determined. They headed for Disney on the appointed day, had the usual amount of fun, snacks, rides, and sunburns, and then headed back to the hotel. That night, Timothy asked her how her day had been. After a few minutes, the little girl answered. "I finally got to go to Disney World. But it wasn't because I was good; it was because I'm yours."

We are part of the body of Christ not because we're good, beautiful, or strong. We are part of it not because of what we do, or what we produce. We are members of this body because we belong to Christ. All of us. We are meant to see each other with compassion, the way God sees each one of us, and all of us. Even the nose hairs.

In Jesus' name, Amen.

Prayer:
Patient God, we are slow to learn that we belong to you, and quick to judge who belongs and who doesn't. Help us, we pray, to find our place in the body of your people, to know our worth and our needs, and to lean on one another. Teach us to see with compassion and to live with understanding. In Jesus' name, Amen.

Like A Layer Cake Of Holiness

After Christmas, the church calendar celebrates the presentation of Jesus in the temple, according to the customs of his Jewish faith. The law required this to occur forty days after the child's birth, and so the church observes this day forty days after Christmas.

Since, therefore, the children share flesh and blood, he himself likewise shared the same things, so that through death he might destroy the one who has the power of death, that is, the devil, and free those who all their lives were held in slavery by the fear of death. For it is clear that he did not come to help angels, but the descendants of Abraham. Therefore he had to become like his brothers and sisters in every respect, so that he might be a merciful and faithful high priest in the service of God, to make a sacrifice of atonement for the sins of the people. Because he himself was tested by what he suffered, he is able to help those who are being tested. (Hebrews 2:14-18)

What's the biggest risk you've ever taken?

Perhaps, unknown to us, you have a secret life in a motorcycle club. Or perhaps you've traveled to unusual places where the danger was part of the thrill. Sky diving? Bungee jumping? Marrying someone you met the week before? Going against your parents' wishes when you chose a college, or a career, or a partner? Starting your own business?

We each have a different tolerance for risk, and what's big to one of us may feel small to others of us. A big risk is an individual choice…but this day in the church calendar makes us realize what a risk-taker God is.

The memory of the baby in the manger is still fresh in our minds as we hear these words from the letter to the Hebrews. We know that Jesus began his life among us as a baby, and now we're forty days from his birth. Thinking about the babies we know, it's a little startling to take in the idea of Jesus as a baby. There's a huge amount of work involved in having a baby around — the crying, the feedings, the diapers, the lack of sleep that wears away at you. All of that was true for Jesus. The writer of Hebrews reminds us that Jesus shared everything that we share.

We all begin the same way.

We begin our lives needing people to take care of us. The infusions of food every few hours, the need for diaper changes, the longing to be held, and the mystery tears that might mean any one of a dozen things. If you have a baby in your life, or had one, then you know how labor-intensive this is. It is also delightful… but the balance of work versus delight is off for a while, until the baby gets bigger.

God took a big risk here, sending the divine presence into the world to start life as a baby. God made a big investment in humanity, coming into our world this way. Along the way, Jesus experienced all of the usual human milestones. He learned to walk, talk, and pray. He had friends, went to synagogue school, and (presumably) learned his father's trade. All the while, there was another layer to his life, of this deep connection with God, and the work God is calling him to do.

As we think about Jesus and his presence in our world, we get to hold both sides of him together. The human being, who started out as a baby, and knew every experience we know. Jesus experienced joy, disappointment, regret, and loss, not to mention hunger, fatigue, and crankiness. And then there's the shimmering presence of God in him. We also recognize the holiness that lived in him, and made God's grace visible through his life.

The human life of Jesus makes a difference in our lives.

Because he was once a baby, we see a little spark of holiness in all babies. Because he spent so much time in prayer, our prayers have an added layer of meaning. Because he connected people around tables, every time we sit at a meal, there's a chance for a deep connection. Because he traveled around with ordinary people and made them part of his work, our ordinary lives are also part of his work.

His incarnation — his human life — gives a layer of holiness to all of human life. Our experiences shine with an echo of his. God means for us never to take our lives for granted. This human life is special enough that Jesus lived one, too. Our world still shimmers with a layer of his presence.

Some years ago, the burden of depression weighed so heavily on my brother that he ended his life by suicide. As some of you know, the grief and disbelief that follow a death by suicide runs deep for all the people touched by such a death. Hard as we try, there's almost no way to make sense of it. The suddenness of the death adds to the grief.

My family, including his cherished wife and young son, and my shell-shocked parents, made our way through the arrangements. We cleaned out his office, and found, to our surprise, that he had put books on hold at the library the day before he died. That added to the puzzle of what he was thinking. We entertained people from out of town, and tried to answer their questions along with our own.

On the day of the funeral, a stranger left a message on my sister-in-law's answering machine, with a name and a number. Overwhelmed by people, she asked me to call him back. Not knowing what he had in mind, I took her telephone out on to her porch, and sat on the front steps to call. I told him who I was, and that I was returning his call to my sister-in-law.

"I wanted to let you know that I was the one who found your brother's body, in the place where he died," he told me. I could only imagine what a terrible experience that was for him. He went on tell me that he was a practitioner of the Sufi religion and had been for forty years. He wanted to let me know that he was going to the place where my brother died every day to say the Sufi prayers for the dead. He would do that for forty days, and then again on the year anniversary.

In a place of complete despair for my brother, his prayers hallowed the ground, and balanced anguish with compassion. It's a mystery that he would be there at that time, but he was, and he used the tools of his faith to ease our grief. In a deserted place, where all hope seemed gone, prayers rose to the God who watches over all of our lives. I think often and with gratitude of this man I never met, who never knew my brother in life, and yet used his faith to add grace to my brother's passing out of this world.

Our lives hold more mystery than we know.

God is present in more places than we can imagine.

The life of Jesus makes our lives holy. His presence lives on in the world in a luminous web of grace, connecting our lives to his life, and to one another. The baby who was born as the Christ child, the man who lived as we live, the redeemer who died for our lives, stays with us still, and all of life is filled with the stunning, risk-taking, abundant presence of God.

In Jesus' name, Amen.

Prayer:

Mighty God, we are overjoyed that you would choose to live in our world, in the form of Jesus. You make the ordinary holy and the everyday transcendent by your presence. Help us to live with awe and reverence, finding you in every part of our lives. With thanksgiving and awe, Amen.

Hold The Candy

As we continue in the season of Epiphany, we hear more of Paul's letter to the Corinthian church. This reading is often read at weddings, and it's fun to consider it as a letter to a whole community, rather than to an individual, or two people.

If I speak in the tongues of mortals and of angels, but do not have love, I am a noisy gong or a clanging cymbal. And if I have prophetic powers, and understand all mysteries and all knowledge, and if I have all faith, so as to remove mountains, but do not have love, I am nothing. If I give away all my possessions, and if I hand over my body so that I may boast, but do not have love, I gain nothing.

Love is patient; love is kind; love is not envious or boastful or arrogant or rude. It does not insist on its own way; it is not irritable or resentful; it does not rejoice in wrongdoing, but rejoices in the truth. It bears all things, believes all things, hopes all things, endures all things.

Love never ends. But as for prophecies, they will come to an end; as for tongues, they will cease; as for knowledge, it will come to an end. For we know only in part, and we prophesy only in part; but when the complete comes, the partial will come to an end. When I was a child, I spoke like a child, I thought like a child, I reasoned like a child; when I became an adult, I put an end to childish ways. For now we see in a mirror, dimly, but then we will see face to face. Now I know only in part; then I will know fully, even as I have been fully known. And now faith, hope, and love abide, these three; and the greatest of these is love. (1 Corinthians 13)

Love it or hate it, Valentine's Day is right around the corner. We're surrounded by hearts and ads for flowers, balloons, and candy to take to your beloved. If you haven't been to the card store yet, this is your reminder. You're welcome.

So do you love it or hate it?

Do you love the emphasis on celebrating the people in your life, the pink cupcakes, the candy, the surprise gifts, the cards where something unexpected is revealed from someone very familiar?

Or, do you hate the emphasis on happy couples, paired off two by two as you miss someone dear to you, or grieve a break-up? Do you hate the sugar and sweetness that forgets that every real relationship has difficulties as well as joys?

If aliens were to arrive on our planet, they might reasonably guess that the word love applied only to shiny, happy, in-shape, perfect couples, or celebrities getting together. But all of you know that love comes in many shapes and forms...the grown-up son or daughter taking care of a parent through a long illness...the parent who fights every day for the child with special needs...the couple whose misty-eyed honeymoon has given way to decades of learning to accommodate each others' dreams, quirks, and passions...the gay or lesbian couple struggling to be seen in our society.

Paul's letter to the church in the city of Corinth addresses this wider vision of love. Our passage follows a section where he reminds this whole church community to value each other's gifts. Without an array of talents and experiences, the community is one-sided. The lawyers needed to appreciate the artists, and the engineers needed to listen to the poets, the extroverts are balanced by the introverts, the people with disabilities have a lot to teach the rest of us, the athletes need to slow down for the people with walkers, and the teachers needed to appreciate the musicians. Paul is addressing the whole community of the church in this passage. It was not meant for a few individuals in their faith lives, but for the whole community. This passage is sometimes read at weddings and commitment ceremonies where two people promise their lives to each other. At the beginning of their lives together, it can be heard as a hope more than an accomplishment, a promise more than a reality. It's also often read at funerals, celebrating a life fully lived in using one's gifts for others. It has special resonance in those settings, but it also belongs to the whole community of faith.

Paul continues to instruct the church at Corinth about how to live together as people of faith. He reminds us that if we speak with all the learning in the world, but people can't understand us, we're missing the Spirit of God. If we speak in tongues — a hotly debated topic in the church at Corinth — if no one gets the message we are speaking, it's useless. If faith never gets from our head to our heart, we're missing the gift of God within us.

For Paul, love is *both* a gift from God and a choice. Love is not the movie-magic heart fluttering we associate with romance, but the daily choices we make... the ways we act...the repeated way we choose to organize our lives for someone else. As Scott Peck said in the classic book *The Road Less Traveled*, love is work. "Love is not a feeling," he says. He added, "keeping an eye on a four- year- old at the beach, concentrating on the interminable disjointed story told by a six-year-old, teaching a teenager how to drive, truly listening to the tale of your spouse's day…all these tasks are often boring, frequently inconvenient, and always energy-draining. They mean work."

Writer and teacher Jack Kornfield often tells the story of a young man who wanted to join a gang (see story in *After the Ecstasy, the Laundry)*. This young man had to prove himself worthy by shooting someone. He went out and shot someone he didn't even know, killed another young man, and then was caught. He was put on trial and convicted. Every day, the mother of the young man he shot came to the trial and watched him. She glared at him, but never said anything.

At the end of the trial, just before they took him away to jail, the mother looked him in the eye and said, simply, "I'm going to kill you."

After a year or so in prison, the guard told him that he had a visitor. It was this woman, the mother of the young man he killed. He was nervous about seeing her again but he didn't have any other visitors, so he agreed. They talked for a while, and she asked him if he needed anything. She came back to see him again, every few months. He was still nervous, but a little less so each time she came.

Finally, it was time for him to get out and she asked him about his plans. "I have no idea. I don't have any family, or any job prospects." So she contacted a friend of hers, and helped him get a job. Then she asked where he planned to live, and, again, he didn't know.

She offered him her spare room, and he came to stay for a while. She made sure he got up, and got to work. She made sure he had enough to eat.

After a couple of months, she said, "Do you remember that day in court when you were convicted of murdering my son for no reason at all, to get into your gang, and I stood up and said, 'I'm going to kill you?'"

"Yes," he said. "I'll never forget that."

As Jack Kornfield tells it, she said, "I killed that boy. I didn't want a boy who could kill in cold blood like that to continue to exist in this world. So I set about visiting you, bringing you presents, bringing you things, and taking care of you. And now I have let you come into my house, got you a job, and gave you a place to live...I set about changing you, and you're not that same person anymore." I want to know, she said, if you'd like to stay here. "I'm in need of a son, and I want to know if I can adopt you."

He said *yes* and she did.

The feeling of love is never going to be enough.

It's how we live.

It's true at home, and equally true in the church community. We flourish because of the gifts that grow from the work of love. Love is the concrete acts — our choices, our work, and our will. Love has deep patience, and determined kindness, and sees far into the future.

In the name of the God who is love, Amen.

Prayer:
God of love, we praise you for every act of self-giving love, and for your love for us, which surrounds us, holds us up, fills our lives and leads us to you. Help us to live up to this vision of love. In Jesus' name, Amen.

Treasures From The Past

We continue in the season of Epiphany, listening to the words Paul writes to the church in Corinth.
Listen for God speaking.

Now I should remind you, brothers and sisters, of the good news that I proclaimed to you, which you in turn received, in which also you stand, through which also you are being saved, if you hold firmly to the message that I proclaimed to you—unless you have come to believe in vain.

For I handed on to you as of first importance what I in turn had received: that Christ died for our sins in accordance with the scriptures,and that he was buried, and that he was raised on the third day in accordance with the scriptures, and that he appeared to Cephas, then to the twelve. Then he appeared to more than five hundred brothers and sisters at one time, most of whom are still alive, though some have died.Then he appeared to James, then to all the apostles. Last of all, as to someone untimely born, he appeared also to me. For I am the least of the apostles, unfit to be called an apostle, because I persecuted the church of God. But by the grace of God I am what I am, and his grace toward me has not been in vain. On the contrary, I worked harder than any of them—though it was not I, but the grace of God that is with me.

Whether then it was I or they, so we proclaim and so you have come to believe. (1 Corinthians 15:1-11)

When my dad was cleaning out our childhood house, he went carefully through each cabinet and box. He thought hard about what to do with everything. My parents were savers so this was a big job. They believed that you never knew when you might need something again, and so their grandkids were delighted to find their parents' childhood toys in the basement whenever they visited. There was a lot for him to sort through.

Each time I visited, I would notice a brown cardboard box sitting next to the door. At the end of the visit, my dad would announce that the box was for me. When I got home, I would find some vintage dish towels, wedding gifts that were never used, or a dish from his parents' home, now mine to use, or some books he thought I would enjoy.

At one point, my usually accommodating husband announced, "No more boxes."

I couldn't just throw out these things my dad was giving me. I would put the new box in the trunk of my car and it would ride around with me for a while, reminding me of my dad. Eventually, I would figure out what to do with the gifts inside.

There's a lot of talk now about how people don't want their parents' treasures anymore. There's a different feeling about possessions, and people live in small apartments or the family home longer. They don't want or need fine china for twenty, or the antique flour sifter that came from great-grandma. Parents and grandparents become dismayed that no one wants their treasures.

It's not the actual item that really matters. The gift is the connection to the other people who have used it, treasured it, loved it, and handed it down. Rejecting the items feels like rejecting them.

But our inheritance comes from more than antique tools and well-worn watches, from more than Thanksgiving platters and lace doilies. We also inherit the gifts of hard work, or principle, or a knack for listening to people. We receive a talent for making the perfect pie crust. We get a memory for sports statistics or the perfect barbeque recipe. We get a lesson in how to fix things, or how to understand people. We take on all these gifts as part of our inheritance. No matter how we feel about the platters and the watches, these gifts are precious.

Writing to the church in Corinth, Paul goes deeper into this vision of our inheritance.

Paul was a traveling salesperson for Jesus, so he didn't have much stuff. He moved from city to city in the ancient world, staying a few weeks or a few years. He traveled light. What he always carried with him, though, was this gift he had received — the certainty of grace through the life and death and resurrection of Jesus. He had had an experience of Jesus that he could never forget, and it changed his life. He's not one of the original disciples, but he's proud to claim that Jesus appeared to him, too, and gave him this inheritance of faith.

It's odd to think about, but Paul's letters are written down before our four gospels. This is an earlier resurrection story than the ones in our gospels. Paul knows the whole resurrection story, and his part in it. He knows that Jesus *was raised on the third day in accordance with the scriptures, and that he appeared to Cephas, then to the twelve. Then he appeared to more than five hundred brothers and sisters at one time, most of whom are still alive, though some have died. Then he appeared to James, then to all the apostles. Last of all, as to someone untimely born, he appeared also to me.*

This deep knowledge of Jesus, even after his human lifetime was over, changed Paul's life.

I wonder if the same is true for us.

This is our inheritance, too. It's passed on to us through family members and friends who have deep faith. We learn it in Sunday school. It sneaks up on us as we do service projects. Understanding comes through conversations and Bible studies, and maybe even dramatic moments where God is undeniably present.

Does it change our lives the way it changed Paul's?

Let's stop and think for a moment about our spiritual inheritance and what difference it makes in our lives.

Where do you see it your inheritance of faith at your work?

This gift of grace comes to us from generations of faithful people. Sometimes people nurture our faith directly — they teach us what they believe, and get us to youth group, and make sure we're part of a faith community. Other times, we learn our faith as adults; we catch it from other people and take it in as a new-found inheritance, a gift from long-lost family. Either way, it belongs to us, just like Grandpa's stamp collection, our aunt's killer chess talents, and the family recipe for sourdough bread.

Adrienne Minh-Chau Le is the daughter of refugees from Vietnam who fled Vietnam at the end of the war. Before she was born, her mother left on a rickety boat, was captured, lived in a refugee camp, and was sponsored by a church in America to come here as a refugee. When Adrienne tries to understand her mother's hardships, and the danger she lived through, she can hardly fathom a life so different from her own sheltered life in America. As a result of her mother's hard work, and her faith and determination, Adrienne attended and graduated from Yale. As an adult, she wanted to know her mother's story. She finally asked for the details she hadn't wanted to know as a child. Her mother told her all about the flight from Vietnam, and the dangerous time in the refugee camp, and then her journey to America.

She never felt her mother's suffering, she says, even though it was part of her heritage. Writing about the legacy of courage and strength she inherited from her mother, she said, "You have always told me that my blood is your blood, that my bones are your bones. I am you and you are me. Your past is mine, the present is ours, and my future is yours. Everything I do in this life is for you, Mom. I hope you feel that." (from OnBeing.org)

May the same be true for us, in the way we live for Jesus.

On this side of the cross, his blood is our blood now, and his bones are our bones. We carry his spirit within us, as part of our inheritance.

We have an inheritance that comes from our families — it's in the plates and sweaters they leave to us, in the football memorabilia, the handmade doilies and the hand-crafted tables. It's in trophies and old cars, but even more deeply in their legacy of values and beliefs. But our deepest legacy comes from the life of Jesus, and the faith we inherit. May we treasure it, and let it change our lives. In Jesus' name, Amen.

Prayer:
Generous God, we thank you for all that has been passed on to us, reminding us who we are, and where we came from. May we treasure the gifts of wisdom, purpose and truth given to us by loved ones, and by Jesus, our teacher and our redeemer. Amen.

Good News Ahead

Our readings continue with Paul's letter to the Corinthians.

Now if Christ is proclaimed as raised from the dead, how can some of you say there is no resurrection of the dead? If there is no resurrection of the dead, then Christ has not been raised; and if Christ has not been raised, then our proclamation has been in vain and your faith has been in vain. We are even found to be misrepresenting God, because we testified of God that he raised Christ—whom he did not raise if it is true that the dead are not raised. For if the dead are not raised, then Christ has not been raised. If Christ has not been raised, your faith is futile and you are still in your sins. Then those also who have died in Christ have perished. If for this life only we have hoped in Christ, we are of all people most to be pitied.

But in fact Christ has been raised from the dead, the first fruits of those who have died. (1 Corinthians 15:12-20)

Church life has a fair amount of certainty.

Our governing board will meet once a month, except in July. We will need to order more cups and coffee several times a year. On 499 out of 500 Sundays, we will have worship on Sunday morning, canceling only if there's a huge storm. On Palm Sunday, we will sing "All Glory, Laud, and Honor" and on Christmas Eve, we will sing "Silent Night." We will have lilies on Easter and poinsettias on Christmas Eve.

There are some mysteries, of course, and there's always a little surprise or two when something big breaks and needs to be fixed. But a lot of our life together unfolds in familiar ways. And we like it that way!

For many years, I worked as a hospice chaplain, and there was a lot less certainty there. I could make a schedule every day, but it would change if there was an emergency, or if someone died. It was really lovely work, helping people come toward death with as much peace as they could manage. I never knew what questions people might have. One day, a young man whose mother was dying asked me something unexpected. Her death was coming fast, and he and his brothers were deeply grieving her passing. She was young to be dying, and they were losing her too soon.

"Will I see my mother again?" he wanted to know.

That may be part of the question that the people of Corinth have for the apostle Paul. We don't know exactly what question from the early church prompted this explanation from Paul. It's like reading the answer from Dear Abby or some other advice column without knowing the question. We can only guess at the answer.

It seems that some of the believers in Corinth were denying that people were raised from death. Perhaps they believed it for Jesus but doubted it for themselves. Paul builds his argument on the belief that Jesus was raised from death.

In this section of his letter to the people in Corinth, he continues the argument that he started in last week's reading. He's proclaiming a truth that he knows from his own experience of meeting the risen Christ. The very same Jesus who lived, taught, told stories, placed his hands on sick people and made them well, ate bread, went away alone to pray in intense conversation with God, got his feet dusty on roads all over Palestine and laughed with his friends over long meals around tables all over Galilee...this very same Jesus was killed, and by God's power, was raised from the dead. Paul's whole argument is built from this belief that Jesus had been raised from death.

For Paul, this is a cornerstone of faith. If this is not true, then our faith is in vain. Jesus was human and had transcended death, by God's power, so the same gift is available for all of us who believe in him. Paul insists here that if the believers denied the resurrection of Jesus, they deny their own hope of resurrection, and let their whole faith slip away.

Paul is working really hard to convince the believers here...but the problem was (as it is today) that there was no proof other than faith. There are so many things in our faith that are uncertain.

When the young man, grieving for his mother as she was dying, asked me if he would see her again, I struggled to know what to say. Years of hospice work had revealed a lot of mystery to me. Person after person seemed to know when they would die. Many of them picked the time of their death. Some needed to be alone. The family sat with them, keeping vigil day after day, but they would choose to die when everyone stepped out for a cup of coffee. Other people waited until everyone was there with them, gathered in the house. Mothers would spare their children, and choose to move out of this life to the next when only the nurse was there. One grandmother hung on through the day of her granddaughter's wedding. She was too weak to be there in person, but she didn't want to ruin her granddaughter's day by dying before the wedding, or even on the day of the wedding. She kept asking the caregiver, "What time is it?" Finally, when it was fifteen minutes past midnight, she had achieved her goal, and she glided right out of this world and into God's embrace.

Person after person saw beloved family and friends, waiting for them, holding out their hands, as if to help them cross over into whatever comes next. "Do you see them?" they would ask. "Do you see who's here?"

"They're not here for me," I would answer, "so I don't need to see them. They're here for you."

After all those years, all I knew to tell the grieving young man was this: "I believe that there are strong connections between this life and whatever we go to next. Love creates bonds between people that death doesn't break. And people seem to get what they need."

Anything more than that we take on faith.

His question has always stayed in the back of my mind, along with the truth of the answer. We get what we need. God is kind like that.

On the morning that my own mother died, there was no surprise. She had been winding down for several days, and everyone who loved her had been there to see her, and to hold her hand one last time. Everyone she loved had gathered around her bed, and spoke words of love and gratitude to her. The morning she died, when I got there before the funeral home came, she had the most wonderful expression on her face. Her face was still, but the expression was one of wonder and amazement, as if she saw something incredibly beautiful in the very last minutes of her life. The last expression on her face was one of delight and joy. No fear, no worry, and no pain. Whatever it was that she saw, it gave me joy to know that she took in some amazing blessing with her very last breaths.

And at the end of the day, after making all the funeral arrangements with my dad, I drove back out of town to go home. I passed an empty storefront that was under construction. There was no clue what was moving in there except one sign that someone has painted on an old, leftover board. In rough painted letters were the words: Coming Soon: Something Better.

That's our faith. We don't know for sure, except that God is abundantly merciful and abundantly kind. We all receive what we need, and much more than we deserve. And in the end, we travel through life on this very same piece of faith. Coming Soon: Something Better.

And so it is. In God's plans, something better is always coming.

In Jesus' name, Amen.

Prayer:
Grace-filled God, we travel in thanksgiving for your gifts in life and death, and for the bonds of love that death cannot break. Your love shatters death for us, and our love carries us toward you and our loved ones who are with you now, until the day we all meet again. In Jesus' name, Amen.

Get Out of the Seed Box

But someone will ask, 'How are the dead raised? With what kind of body do they come?' Fool! What you sow does not come to life unless it dies. And as for what you sow, you do not sow the body that is to be, but a bare seed, perhaps of wheat or of some other grain. But God gives it a body as he has chosen, and to each kind of seed its own body.

So it is with the resurrection of the dead. What is sown is perishable, what is raised is imperishable. It is sown in dishonor, it is raised in glory. It is sown in weakness, it is raised in power. It is sown a physical body, it is raised a spiritual body. If there is a physical body, there is also a spiritual body. Thus it is written, 'The first man, Adam, became a living being'; the last Adam became a life-giving spirit. But it is not the spiritual that is first, but the physical, and then the spiritual. The first man was from the earth, a man of dust; the second man is from heaven. As was the man of dust, so are those who are of the dust; and as is the man of heaven, so are those who are of heaven. Just as we have borne the image of the man of dust, we will also bear the image of the man of heaven.

What I am saying, brothers and sisters, is this: flesh and blood cannot inherit the kingdom of God, nor does the perishable inherit the imperishable. (1 Corinthians 15:35-38, 42-50)

Years ago, when my daughter was a tiny baby, just a couple weeks old, I could already feel the time zipping by. The five-pound newborn had turned into an eight-pound baby, and she already felt different when I held her. I looked into the future and could see the time zipping by. I lamented the speed of life to my dad, and he said, "Well, time only goes one way, honey."

It does only go one way. And it goes quickly.

You know that experience from your own lives, or from the kids you know. From Christmas to summer, your grandkids grow in amazing ways. The kids next door come outside, and it seems like they've grown a foot in the week since you saw them. Kids at church are being baptized one day and going to college the next, or so it seems. At your own house, all of a sudden the kid who couldn't remember to put the top back on the peanut butter is an engineer. The niece or nephew who always lost their shoes is giving you financial advice.

It happens to adults, too, but we notice it less. The changes are more on the inside, and less on the outside. We wake up one day and realize that we're not angry about something any more. Or the worry we've carried around for years has lifted, and we feel years lighter. Or we don't have the desire to eat too much or spend too much or gossip too much anymore.

There are all kinds of growth in our lives. Each one is a kind of rebirth, out of one thing, and into another.

In this letter to the believers in the city of Corinth, Paul is talking about the resurrection that happens at the end of our lives. We await that day, and as we do, we experience this same process all through our lives, until the final resurrection at the end.

Paul uses the image of seeds to make his point. A seed has to die and take a new form to come to fullness. A seed that stays a seed is a little piece of dried-out promise. A seed that falls into the ground, cracks and sprouts can become a flower, or a tree. It can become a redwood, or a sunflower, or a tomato, or a gorgeous lily. There are all kinds of promise in the seed, Paul says, and in us, as the people of God.

The hard part is that promises only come to life when something else lets go and dies. It only goes in one direction.

In her book *Kitchen Table Wisdom*, Rachel Naomi Remen tells about a doctor she knows, named Frank. He's a middle-aged internist, and the director of a clinic. He is a good doctor, but he's thinking about leaving the field of medicine.

One day he is reviewing his notes before he sees Mrs. Gonzalez, one of his patients. She was an elderly woman, in the last stages of breast cancer. He didn't have any further treatment to offer her, so their visits together involved adjusting her medication and making sure she wasn't in pain.

Thinking about the visit, he found — much to his surprise — that it seemed like he should pray with her. He didn't really pray much and this felt like a big risk. Still, when she arrived, he turned to this frail, grandmother and suggested that they pray together. She heard what he said and started to cry.

Taking her hand, he sat and waited.

Finally, she answered him. "That would be very wonderful, doctor." She told him that she was Catholic, and asked if they could kneel down. This unnerved him even more. He glanced at the door to be sure no one would see them. Then he, in his white lab coat, helped her kneel on the floor and he knelt next to her, in the tiny exam room in the clinic.

Mrs. Gonzalez began to pray, speaking first in Spanish and then in English. The doctor had not prayed in years, but he felt a sense of calm settle over him and the sound of her voice called up a prayer from his childhood, one he hadn't thought of for a long time.

Then Mrs. Gonzalez reached across and touched him on the cheek, and began to pray for him and his work. She asked God to bless him and strengthen him in his work.

Six months later, he said he could still feel the light touch of her hand on his face, and he found himself reaching back to that moment when he needed added strength, wisdom, or patience. He thought he was praying for her...and the gift turned out to be for him.

We never know how the seed will sprout and grow. We never know what we need to let go of, to let end, to let die in our lives, so something new can be born. But in God's world, we get to choose. We can stay stuck in the seed, dried up, but still full of promise. Or we can accept God's promise of birth into something new, and let go of the old. We can step into resurrection after resurrection, letting each seed within us flower into something new. Or we can stay where we are all dried up in the seed box.

God is a gardener who doesn't force the growth but is always willing to plant us somewhere, to water the seeds within us with experiences that nurture us, to bring the bright light of wisdom to our growth.

God is always ready to grow something new in us, when we can let the seed go and sprout. That pattern is true for our whole lives, and comes to fullness at the end of life.

Thanks be to God. Amen.

Prayer:

God who is the gardener of our lives, we give you thanks for every place of resurrection in our lives. Every place where something ends and a new thing begins happens by your grace. Every death that leads to resurrection is from your care. Keep us faithful to you as resurrection people, we pray. In Jesus' name, Amen.

Without The Mask

This Sunday, Transfiguration Sunday, comes to us as the end of the Epiphany season, and as the doorway to the season of Lent. We have another piece of Paul's writing to the people of Corinth.

Listen for God speaking.

Since, then, we have such a hope, we act with great boldness, not like Moses, who put a veil over his face to keep the people of Israel from gazing at the end of the glory that was being set aside. But their minds were hardened. Indeed, to this very day, when they hear the reading of the old covenant, that same veil is still there, since only in Christ is it set aside. Indeed, to this very day whenever Moses is read, a veil lies over their minds; but when one turns to the Lord, the veil is removed. Now the Lord is the Spirit, and where the Spirit of the Lord is, there is freedom. And all of us, with unveiled faces, seeing the glory of the Lord as though reflected in a mirror, are being transformed into the same image from one degree of glory to another; for this comes from the Lord, the Spirit.

Therefore, since it is by God's mercy that we are engaged in this ministry, we do not lose heart. We have renounced the shameful things that one hides; we refuse to practice cunning or to falsify God's word; but by the open statement of the truth we commend ourselves to the conscience of everyone in the sight of God. (2 Corinthians 3:12-4:2)

One of the greatest television shows ever was the series "Lie to Me," which featured a scientist who can read micro-expressions. These are the tiny movements of the face — the "leakage," as he calls it, of our true emotions. Most of the time, we present socially acceptable emotions, but our true feelings sneak out of us, in spite of ourselves. These expressions come and go in a fraction of a second.

It may be that I'm the only person who ever loved this show because it wasn't around for long...but it was still fascinating to watch the team of people on the show interpret faces, and find the truth each week.

The television show was based on the real-life scientist Dr. Paul Ekman, who pioneered the science of micro-expressions. In the show, these experts in faces consult with the FBI, various police departments, and big companies, all using the science of reading faces. These expressions come and go so quickly, in a fraction of a second, that most people can't see them. We see what people want to show us...what they want us to see.

But if you could read those tiny moments of truth on the human face, you would have a knowledge that most of us lack.

In this section of his letter to the church in Corinth, Paul talks about reading faces, too. This is Transfiguration Sunday, a Sunday when we talk about the revelation of the divine aspect of Jesus. Paul recalls Moses going up the mountain to meet God. After the meeting, Moses' face shone with God's glory. It was so bright that the people could not stand it. The people begged Moses to cover it up. One writer (Scott Hoezee) calls it "a holy sunburn." Moses had to wear a covering over his face — his encounter with God changed him in a visible way.

But Paul says, "there's no need for that kind of veil." Thanks to Jesus, we can see God's glory directly, without a veil, without being shielded. Because of Jesus, the glory of God is visible in the world — ready for us to take it in. We don't have to wonder and guess about God anymore. The bright light of God's glory is right out there for us all to see, visible in the world, thanks to Jesus.

God's glory is alive among us. Our connection can be visible on our faces, too. Thanks to the example of Jesus, we can see the glory of God whenever we want to.

But it still comes in micro-expressions.

That glory lives in the world — but we have to watch for it.

When my daughter, Lucy, started running high school cross country, I met a whole different kind of parenting philosophy. For me, kids' sports are about teamwork and having fun, but I realize that some people take it much more seriously. At the very first high school meet, I was standing with some parents, cheering for all the kids. Some of them finished the race, and one mother looked at her watch and said, "Oh, my son is not going to be happy with his time."

She was right. Those boys are impressive runners, but the person who impressed me the most, in all the meets, was a girl named Callie.

High school cross country, as many of you know, is about running three miles. It takes about twenty minutes, if you're quick, or thirty or forty for some runners. The fast ones are impressive, but the slow ones really dazzle me. They're there, not because they're good at it, but for some other reason.

At one race, I watched all the women runners take off in a fast cloud of long, teenage legs and ponytails... and then saw a girl with braces on both legs start walking, step by slow step. She was at the next race, too, and something about her spirit and character came through loud and clear. It wasn't a micro-expression. She was more on the macro end. When she rounded the corner, and the crowd was gone, I asked her, "Do you mind if I walk with you for a while?"

"That's fine," she said.

I told her my name, and she told me hers. Callie. Callie, with the braces on both legs, turned out to be the most grounded, thoughtful teenager I've met in a long time. She talked about her work in the drama club, her parents and the advice they give her, and her work as a peer counselor. The next race, she talked about school, and I found myself hoping that the kids at her school could see past the veil of the outside to the interesting person inside.

I know at least one person did. When the cross country season started the next year, when I saw her the next year, at the first race of the season, she told me about her boyfriend. And then she didn't need me to walk with her anymore because he was doing it. I was a little sad because I enjoyed talking to her so much, but also thrilled that someone could see the inside of her. Someone had read her face properly and saw her value.

In the speedy world of cross country, Callie didn't look like much. Other kids were crossing the finish line while she still labored along the track. But on the inside there was glory. Over time, she let that spirit shine out.

The glory of God shone out from her, for the people who remembered to look.

We're all like that.

We may not look like much in a world obsessed with movie stars and full of admiration for athletes. To my knowledge, none of us are tech billionaires, supermodels or Wall Street wizards. But we have all the spark and talent that God gave us, on the inside. We have all our hard-won wisdom under the surface. We all have a little bit of God's glory in us.

We reflect the glory of Jesus, our redeemer. His presence lives in us, and shines out from us, when we let it.

The challenge is both to shine with God's glory, and to see it in each other.

God's glory is alive in the world, when we pay attention. When we watch for the little moments, we find God's glory all around us. God is still at work, and if we watch carefully, we will find the presence of God all around us. No veil. No hidden presence. Right here with us.

But it comes in micro-moments, and micro-visions, so we have to watch. If we watch each other closely, we will see glory blaze up and shine out. If we watch closely, the glory of God shines among us, and within us.

We are more than we know, by the grace of God. Thanks be to God for Jesus, who revealed the fullness of God to us, and for all the people and moments that lift the veil and show us the truth.

In Jesus' name, Amen.

Prayer:

Loving God, we don't see as we ought to see, and our eyes are often closed to your glorious presence. Still, hope rises in us, and we pray that you would transform us into people who can see truly, and live rightly. In Jesus' name, Amen.

CPSIA information can be obtained
at www.ICGtesting.com
Printed in the USA
FFHW022020281018
48979908-53230FF